ROCKY THE RESCUE
A Collection of Happy Travel Tales

ROCKY THE RESCUE
A Collection of Happy Travel Tales ©

Written by Jane Justice Park
Illustrated by Jeanine-Jonee

Published by

Be sure to look for the audio version of this book. Message us at
www.ROCKYTHERESCUE.com or **www.JANEJUSTICEPARK.com**.
Story written by and concept images by Jane Justice Park
Cover and book illustrations by Jeanine-Jonee

ISBN
979-8-9852751-6-2

Library of Congress Control Number

To my Heavenly Father who created all creatures great and small with magnanimous love.

"To honor my parents Michael and Diane Park and my big brother Jason who shows me how beautiful and healing a God-blessed family can be. I'm humbled and grateful to share divine, strengthening joy and love with grace to overcome all challenges with eternity set in our united hearts."

♥ *Jane*

Rocky Bear

TRAVEL PLANS
READ LEFT ➡ RIGHT

BOARDING PASS

DOG TO MEET 
CHIHUAHUA
ROCKY BEAR AIRLINES
FROM AMERICA TO MEXICO
PAGE 06

BOARDING PASS

DOG TO MEET
BRAZILIAN MASTIFF
ROCKY BEAR AIRLINES
FROM MEXICO TO BRAZIL
PAGE 07

BOARDING PASS

DOG TO MEET 
SPINONE ITALIANO
ROCKY BEAR AIRLINES
FROM BRAZIL TO ITALY
PAGE 08

BOARDING PASS

DOG TO MEET
DALMATION
ROCKY BEAR AIRLINES
FROM ITALY TO CROATIA
PAGE 09

BOARDING PASS

DOG TO MEET 
FRENCH POODLE
ROCKY BEAR AIR
FROM CROATIA TO FRANCE
PAGE 10

BOARDING PASS

DOG TO MEET
RUSSIAN BORZOI
ROCKY BEAR AIRLINES
FROM FRANCE TO RUSSIA
PAGE 11

BOARDING PASS

DOG TO MEET 
SHARPEI
ROCKY BEAR AIRLINES
FROM RUSSIA TO CHINA
PAGE 14

BOARDING PASS

DOG TO MEET
JAPANESE CHIN
ROCKY BEAR AIRLINES
FROM CHINA TO JAPAN
PAGE 15

BOARDING PASS

DOG TO MEET 
JINDO
ROCKY BEAR AIRLINES
FROM JAPAN TO KOREA
PAGE 16

BOARDING PASS

DOG TO MEET
BASENJI
ROCKY BEAR AIRLINES
FROM KOREA TO KENYA
PAGE 20

BOARDING PASS

DOG TO MEET 
CANAAN DOG
ROCKY BEAR AIRLINES
FROM KENYA TO ISRAEL
PAGE 21

BOARDING PASS

DOG TO MEET
ARMENIAN GAMPR
ROCKY BEAR AIRLINES
FROM ISRAEL TO ARMENIA
PAGE 22

BOARDING PASS

DOG TO MEET 
NORWEGIAN ELKHOUND
ROCKY BEAR AIRLINES
FROM ARMENIA TO NORWAY
PAGE 23

BOARDING PASS

TRAVEL HOST
TERRIER MIXED
ROCKY BEAR AIRLINES
FROM NORWAY TO AMERICA

Hi!

BOW WOW... I'm ROCKY THE RESCUE! WOOF WOOF! BOW WOW!

Because I am a d-o-g, DOG, that is how I speak. In America, doggies like me go WOOF WOOF and BOW WOW ...and that is called our bark.

Can you bark like me?

WOOF WOOF BOW WOW!

I HAVE SO MUCH TO SHARE WITH YOU BECAUSE YOU ARE MY BESTEST FRIEND. WOULD YOU LIKE TO MEET MY DOGGIE FRIENDS? THEY ARE FROM ALL OVER THE WORLD! WE ALL SPEAK DIFFERENT LANGUAGES, BUT WE CAN ALL BE GOOD FRIENDS. ARE YOU READY? OKAY~! *LET'S GO!*

This country borders America below, so on our trip, we will pass first through Mexico.

In Mexico, my dog pals are called PERROS. In Mexico, PERROS bark

GUAU GUAU!

How do PERROS speak? Si! Yes! PERROS bark

GUAU GUAU!

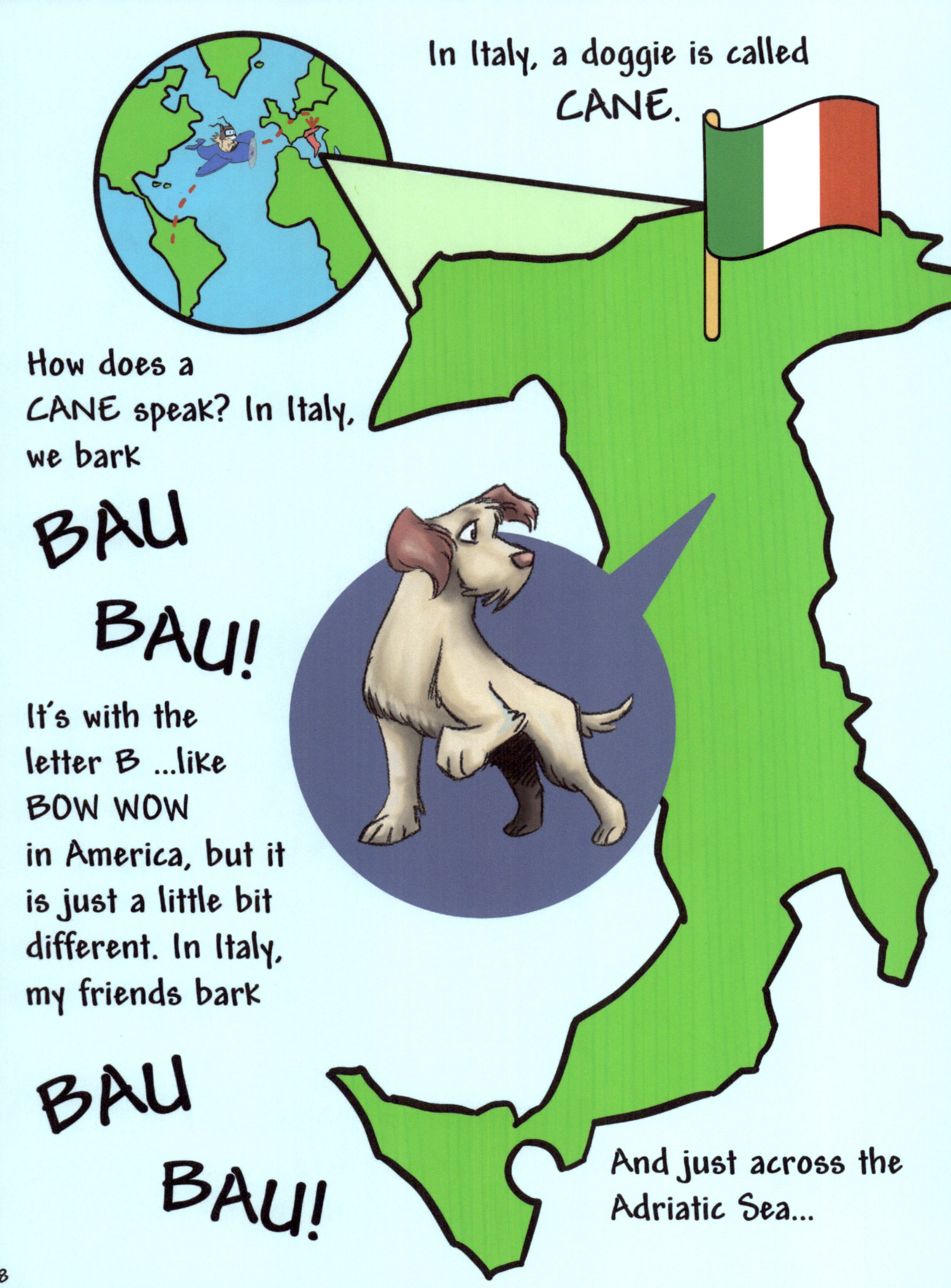

In Italy, a doggie is called CANE.

How does a CANE speak? In Italy, we bark

BAU BAU!

It's with the letter B ...like BOW WOW in America, but it is just a little bit different. In Italy, my friends bark

BAU BAU!

And just across the Adriatic Sea...

In Croatia, a doggie is called
PAS.

My friends in Croatia bark

VAU VAU VAU

Let's try that together:

VAU VAU!

In Croatia, a PAS like me barks how?

In France a dog is called **Un CHIEN.**

Un CHIEN says

WOUF WOUF

What is my friend in France called?
Un CHIEN—Oui Oui!

Yes!

Good job!

In France, Un CHIEN barks

WOUF WOUF

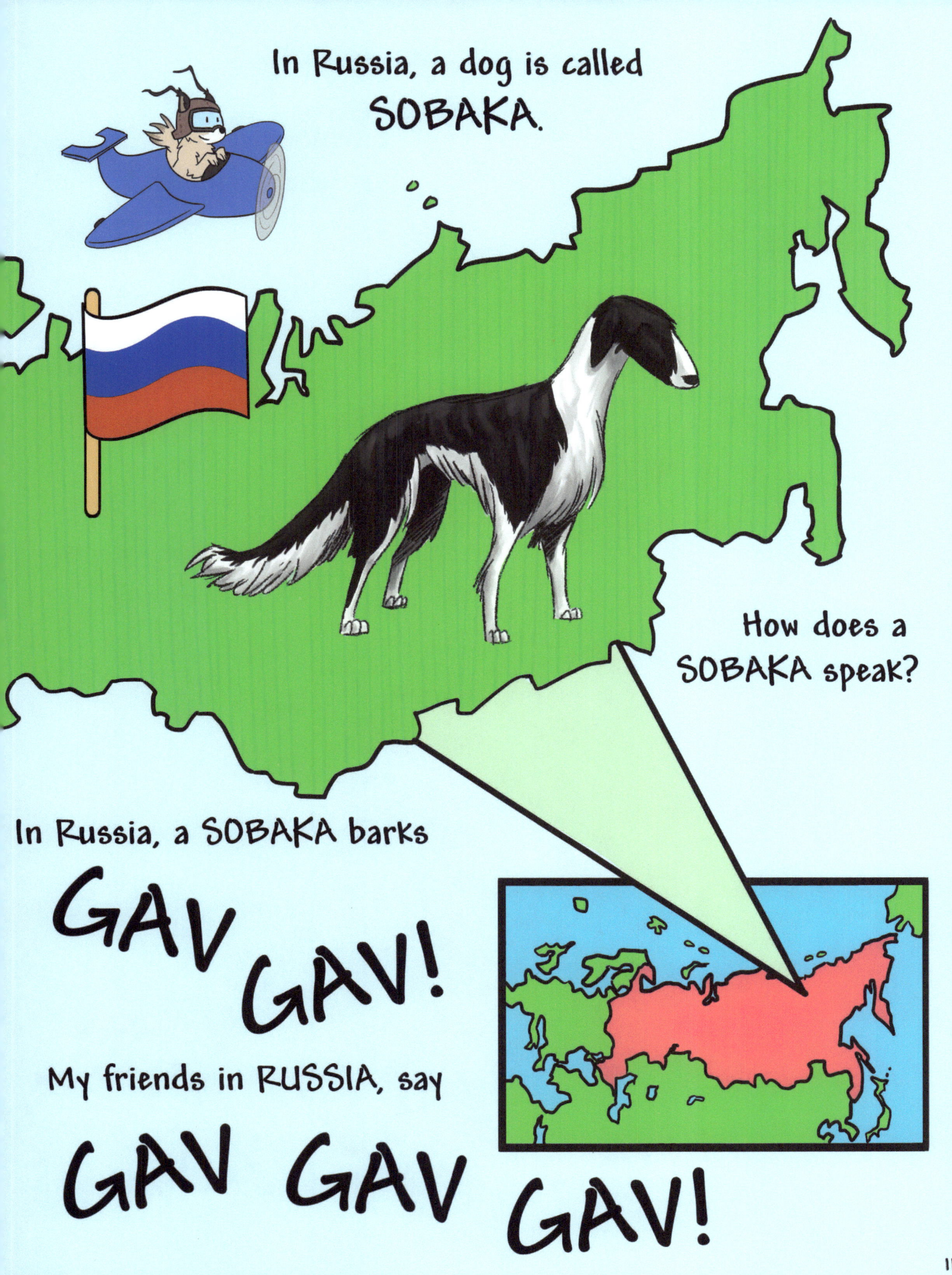

In Russia, a dog is called SOBAKA.

How does a SOBAKA speak?

In Russia, a SOBAKA barks

GAV GAV!

My friends in RUSSIA, say

GAV GAV GAV!

PAWESOME

This is so much fun. East Asia here we come!

By the way, I packed healthy snacks to share.

I woof to eat sweet potatoes, rice and beans, and carrots with peanut butter. Yummy fun!

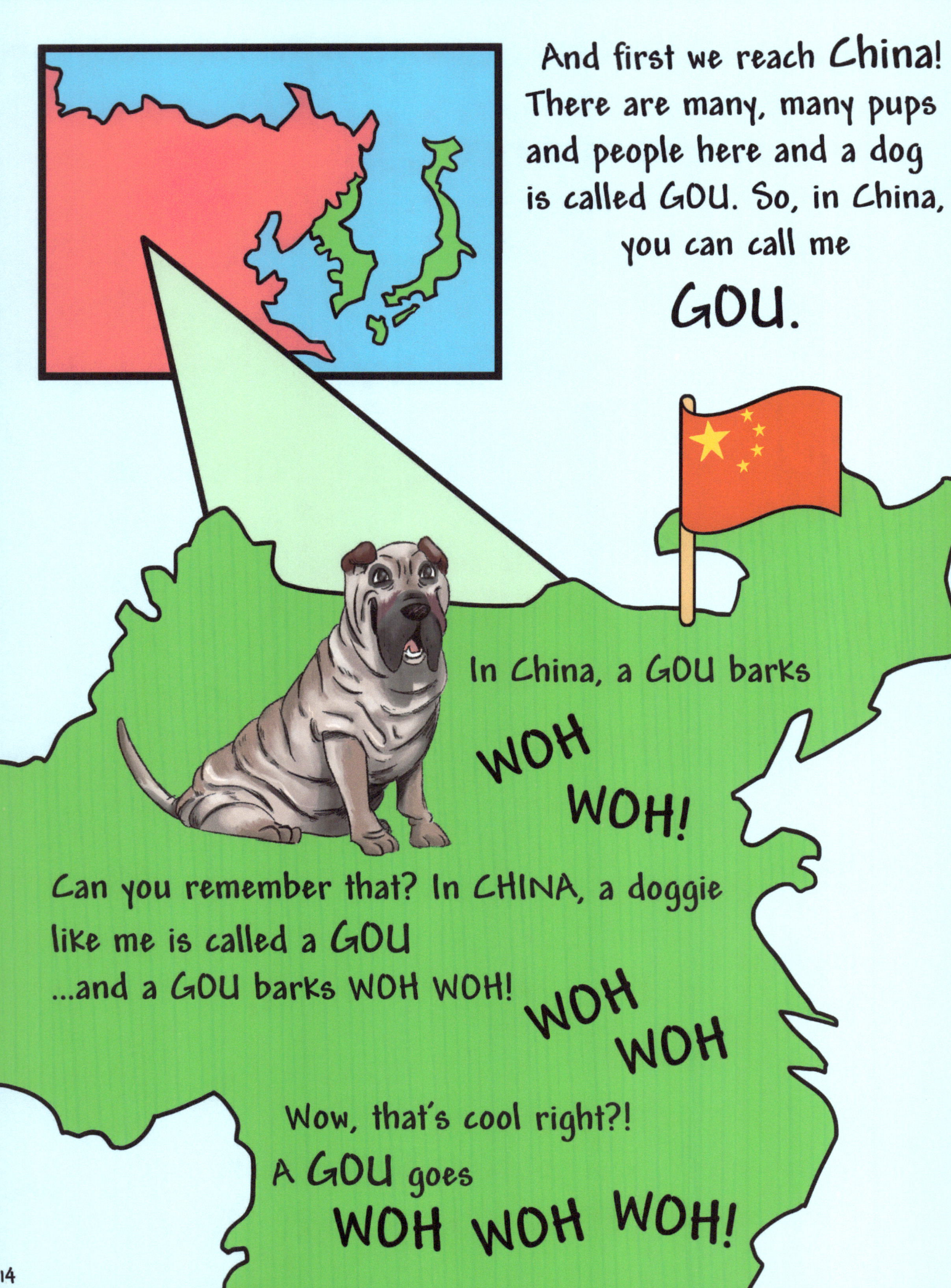

And first we reach China! There are many, many pups and people here and a dog is called GOU. So, in China, you can call me GOU.

In China, a GOU barks WOH WOH!

Can you remember that? In CHINA, a doggie like me is called a GOU ...and a GOU barks WOH WOH!

WOH WOH

Wow, that's cool right?! A GOU goes WOH WOH WOH!

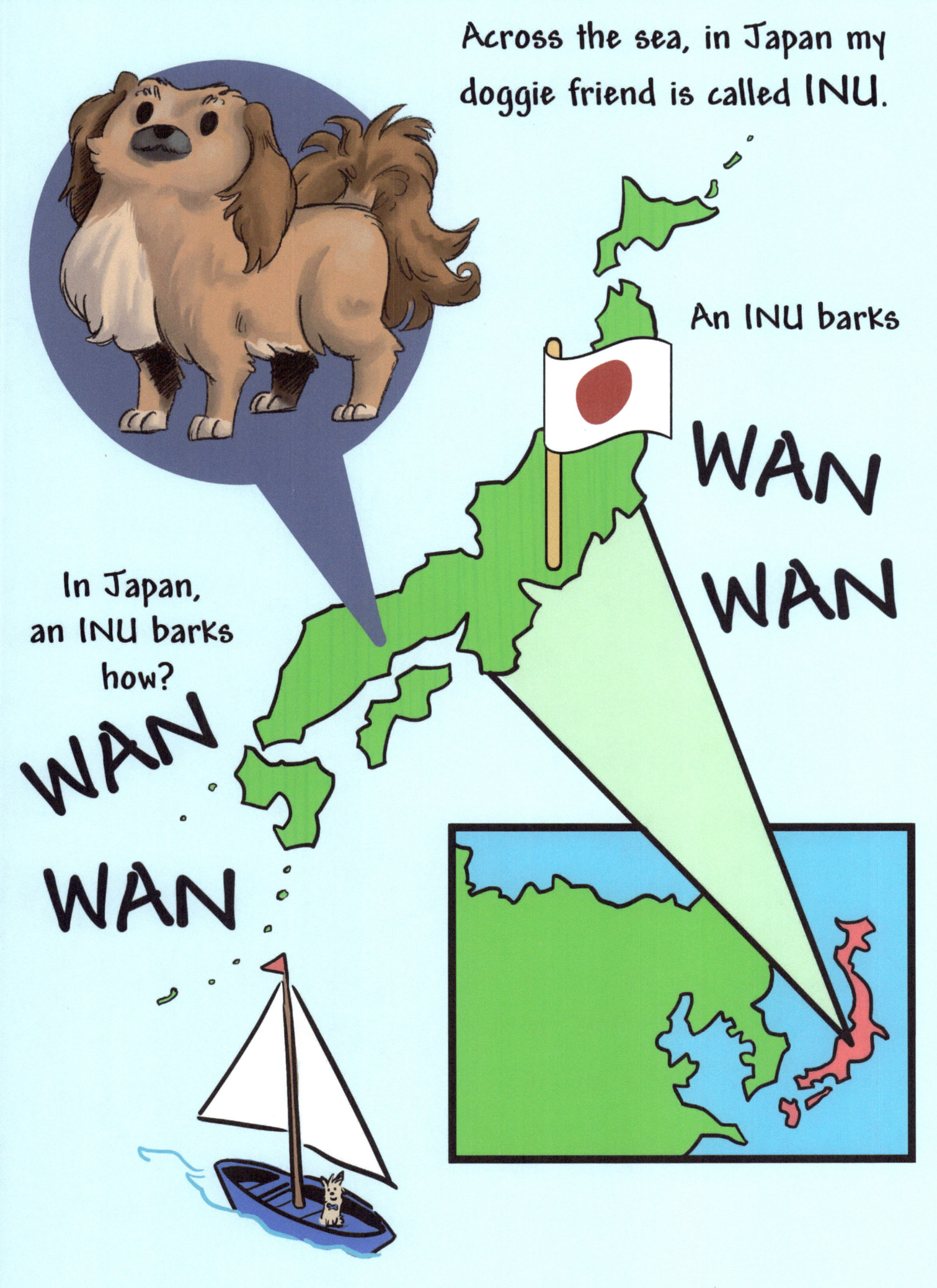

South Korea is a super special place. It's where my sister is from!

Meet Tessa.

Tessa is also a rescue pup saved by good humans like you!

She was so sad at the scary dog meat farm she was rescued from. Now, she is happy with me in our fur-ever home!

My human mom and my sister Tessa were born in South Korea.

Tessa's breed is JINDO and she barks like this:

MUNG
MUNG
MUNG!

In Korea, my sister and I are called GHAE and we speak by barking

MUNG MUNG!

I miss my family...

...and the adventures we have back home.

Family is so special and so we stop by Kenya.
I have a human family member there! My human mom sponsored* a child I hope to meet one day.

For now, I learned pups in Kenya are called MBWA and bark like this: WUH WUH!

WUH WUH!

WUH WUH!

(*Sponsored through an organization called World Vision.)

"Sponsoring a child is an ongoing commitment to help meet the child's basic needs by investing in their community and building a relationship until they or their community become independent."

In Israel, a dog friend is called KELEV.

They bark with an H sound, too. H like in the word Happy.

HAV HAV!

Can you remember their happy bark in Israel? Hooray!

HAV HAV HAV!

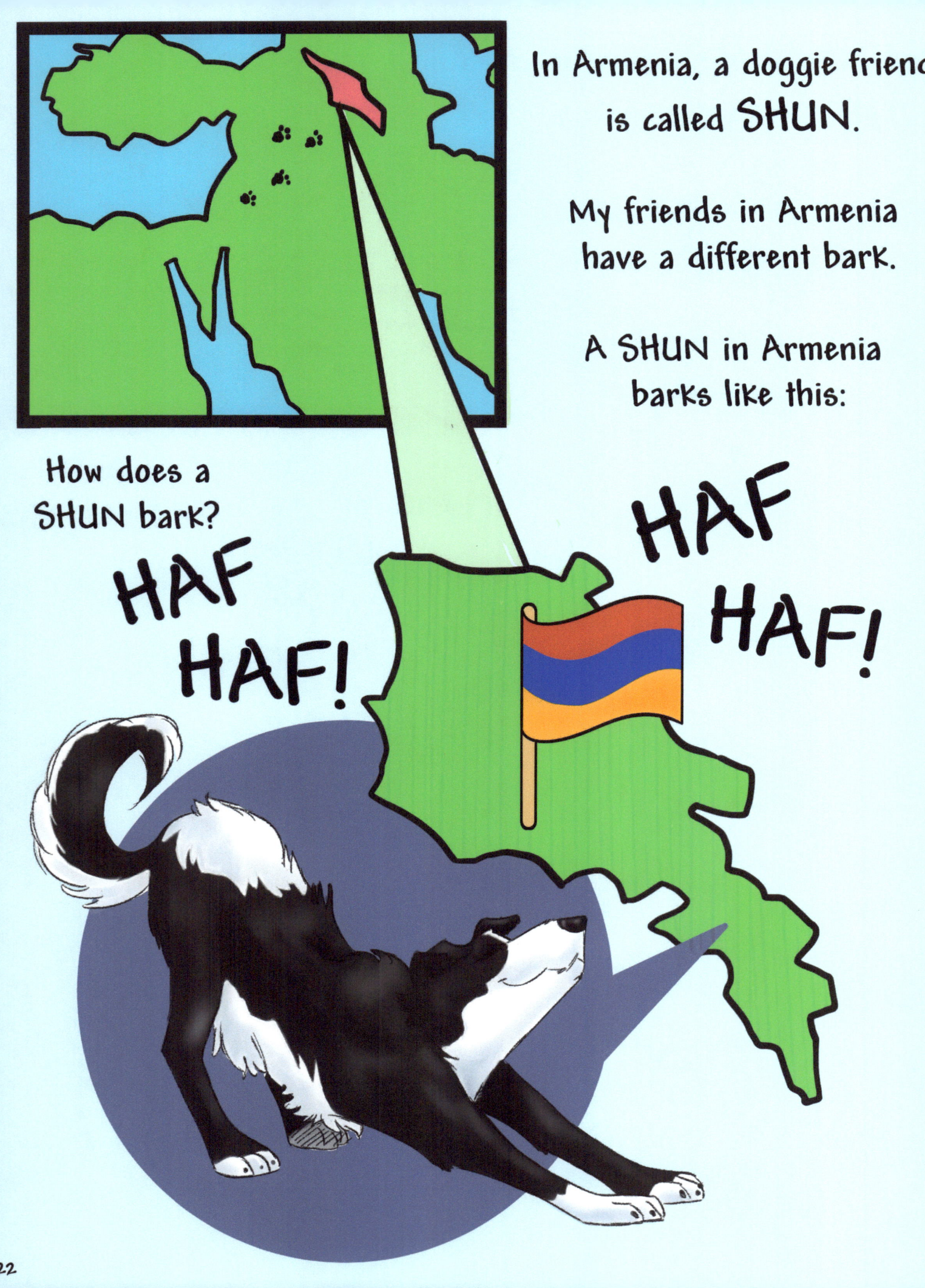

Now we are in Norway.

Here, I am called HUND and bark like this:

VOFF VOFF!

As we leave Norway, how should I bark my goodbye?

Very Nice with a V! In Norway, I say

VOFF VOFF!

All around the world, we look and sound a little different, but I hope you can hear our hearts. What we mean to say to you is the same: "You are my friend and I WOOF you!"~ oopsie! I meant to say it how we in America speak: When I say, "I WOOF you," I really mean I LOVE you.

Thank you for being my friend. I **WOOF WOOF** you.

I **LOVE LOVE** you very, very much for you are my bestest friend.

We are home sweet home now.
Thank you for being my travel buddy and bestest friend.
I hope we keep in touch FUR-EVER!

Tell me about your dreams...

where do you want to travel next?

What healthy treat can
we share next time?

ABOUT ROCKY

Rocky Bear (aka Rocky the Rescue) and his family are devoted to celebrating the blessing of life. With 90% of proceeds of his first book going to support animal rescue efforts, this illustrated book in your hand expands the world's most creative and charitable canine's ability to help his pup-peers find their own fur-ever family. So thank you for being a part of giving back with love. Gratitude always to the volunteers with Dogs Without Borders (www.dogswithoutborders.org) who found Rocky in a trash bag with his siblings on an L.A. street when he was so young that he barely filled two cupped human hands. Stay in touch with Rocky and his family on his website www.ROCKYTHERESCUE.com

CONTESSA & DOG MEAT FARMS

Contessa Bear (aka Tessa) found her way to becoming Rocky's bigger, but younger little sister… through the brave caring hands of a global network of animal advocates. Just like industrialized meat farms in countries like America raise animals including cows, pigs, and chickens in unnatural, unsanitary, and unkind factory farms, Tessa was born on a farm just for dog meat. She could have become the main ingredient in a Korean stew, but activists from Save Korean Dogs (www.savekoreandogs.org) and Wags and Walks (www.wagsandwalks.org) saved and sent her to the United States.

Since finding her new family, Tessa has worked hard to let go of her fears learned at the scary dog meat farm where fellow pups suffered brutal injuries and neglect by people who didn't understand how much trauma their torturous actions could cause. Some pups are so wounded, they never recover and some like Tessa, find a space to become the happy, well-trained, and free pups they were created to be. Tessa is learning to trust not just one or two, but many humans who have a tender way toward her. By supporting Rocky and Tessa's book, you are being a part of ending the dog and cat meat trade worldwide--THANK YOU... We WOOF you!

WORLD VISION

This global-Christian relief development and advocacy organization is dedicated to working with children, families, and communities to overcome poverty and injustice.

If you are interested in sponsoring a child, your gracious commitment can change not only one child's life, but the family's and larger community's outlook as well. Rocky's mom, Jane, sponsored a human child in Kenya and enjoys writing to and receiving letters from those in that African village. Your foster child can be from almost any region in the world! What a way to grow your impact as a global citizen!

www.WVI.org
www.worldvision.org

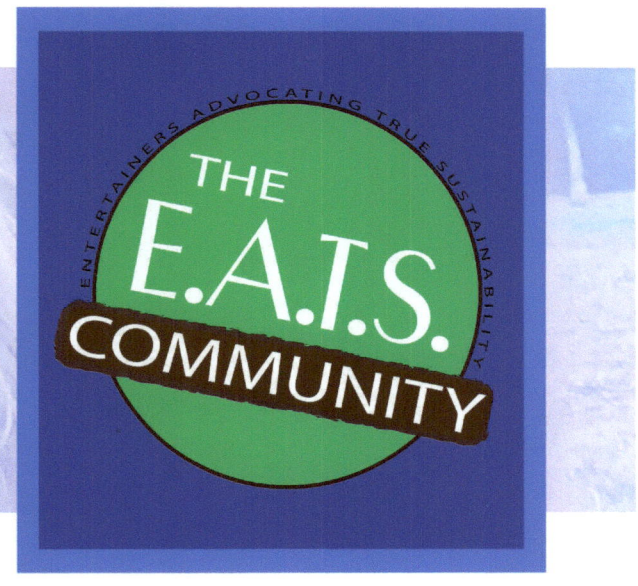

THE E.A.T.S. COMMUNITY

This is a personal and professional philanthropic venture to help heal people and our planet by cultivating a taste for whole, nutritionally rich, minimally processed food. From 60 second comedic films, to in-classroom motivational lessons on food and filmmaking, to simple tips or recipes online, this outreach aims to #makeyouhungryforhealthyin60seconds.

E.A.T.S. stands for: Entertainers Advocating True Sustainability. And so this passion project melds food justice, the arts, and community involvement with purpose into our social media driven world.

Get hungry for healing food, well-balanced living, and delicious treats at: www.EATScommunity.org
& IG: @eatscommunity

ABOUT THE AUTHOR

A consummate ARTivist, Jane enjoys turning every endeavor into an artistic force for good and is especially conscious of harnessing the power of language to infuse the world with hope.

As well as being a children's book author, Jane Justice Park is an actress, martial artist, healthy food lover, model, and speaker with diverse film and television credits. Having earned a presidential honor for her charitable community activism, Jane seeks to serve and speak out for the voiceless and oppressed, worldwide. Her inspirational first non-fiction book Rocky the Rescue gives 90% to animal rescue organizations and the book in your hands now is a passion project that came together by faith.

Having overcome great health challenges, Jane now utilizes the insight gained from her healing journey to help others in their journeys toward wholeness. Health advocacy, life coaching, and artistic expression play a big part in her prayerful ministry. She is led by her mission statement: "Rescue the lost, heal the hurting, speak up for those who cannot." Her heart, hands, feet, and every aspect of her life are led by this directive. All her books offer special ways to share her Spirit-filled calling to love all, always.

Jane is grateful for the most resilient, compassionate, and pure hearted people she gets to call mom, dad, and big brother (Diane, Michael, and Jason Park) as well as those who are dearest friends-like-family who are true gifts from God.
www.JANEJUSTICEPARK.com

We also want to list some other global animal rescue organizations working to save other furry friends like Tessa.
www.animalsasia.org ~ www.careanimalrights.org ~ www.changeforanimals.org ~
www.HSI.org ~ www.soidog.org

Also, it is important to note--not all dog meat comes from being raised en-masse on farms, many are strays from the street or companion animals stolen from their humans. We will celebrate the day all cruelty to animals comes to an end and we invite you to be part of this move toward mercy and justice.

Thank you for joining Rocky the Rescue on this adventure! If you would like to join Jane Justice Park's fan club and receive a freebie now and then, go to the website below or scan the QR code.

https://dl.bookfunnel.com/hnjgbstilt

Other books by Jane:
Rocky the Rescue: A Collection of His Rescue Tales (Non-fiction stories)
Shyla the Trailblazing Super Snail (Easy Readers 4-8 y.o.)